THE STAGE OF POWER

ISBN: 9798875926785

DEDICATION

I dedicate this book to all those who seek to understand the complexities of power and politics, in the hope that these words may illuminate their own paths.

TABLE OF CONTENTS

PREFACE

Within these pages, we embark on a journey through the intricate web of political power. This preface is an invitation to explore the corridors of government, unravel betrayals, and discover the moral dilemmas that permeate the stage of power.

ACKNOWLEDGMENTS

I sincerely thank all who contributed to the realization of this work. To my family, friends, and mentors, whose support and inspiration were essential. To the dedicated team that worked tirelessly to bring these pages to life, my profound gratitude.

PROLOGUE

The first page of this work inaugurates a philosophical and sociological exploration of the president's discourse, opening the doors to the fertile ground of the stage of power. This prologue establishes the foundations for a deeper analysis of human complexities, leadership, and society that will unfold in the following pages.

INTRODUCTION

The first page of this philosophical and sociological journey transports us to the heart of the president's discourse. His words, like a portal, invite us to enter the stage of power, an arena where the essence of leadership and its impact on society are masterfully presented. This discourse is not just a set of words; it is the opening of a profound dialogue on human complexity.

The stage of power, outlined by every expression and intonation of the president, becomes fertile ground for the sowing of reflections and questioning. It is in this symbolic space that the seeds of critical thoughts are planted, creating roots that will extend throughout the book. Leadership, as represented in this discourse, reveals itself as a multifaceted phenomenon, capable of shaping society in unexpected ways.

This is the prologue to our broader exploration of human complexity. The stage of power, shaped by the president's words, is not just a physical location but a metaphor alive for the intersection between discourse and human complexity.

CHAPTER 1
THE CURTAIN RISES

The sun began to cast its rays over the city, but in the corridors of power, the truth remained in the shadows. In this scenario of political intrigues, the curtain was rising, revealing the backstage of the government, a world where loyalty was a rare commodity, and alliances were made and broken as swiftly as the wind.

In the heart of this turmoil, President Martinez spoke, his carefully chosen words not only conveying a message to the nation but weaving a web of strategies that would shape the political destiny of all present. The stage was set, and the characters, each with their political masks, eagerly awaited the next act.

While the audience listened attentively, behind the scenes, Senator Vasquez read between the lines of the speech. He knew that the words spoken at that podium were not just rhetoric; they were seeds planted to influence minds and garner support. The battle for public opinion had already begun.

At the end of the speech, the meeting room transformed into a playing field, where looks and fake smiles hid dark intentions. The curtain had risen, revealing a panorama where politics was a three-dimensional chess game, where victory depended not only on moves but on the ability to anticipate the opponent's next steps.

As the chapter came to a close, it became clear that, in the city governed by the spotlight, it was behind the scenes that the real machinations occurred. The curtain had risen, but the show had just begun.

CHAPTER 2
INTRIGUES AND ALLIANCES

In the halls of power, intrigues simmered like a pot about to boil over. Each character, motivated by secret ambitions, tried to decipher the moves of the other, creating a complex dance of temporary alliances and calculated betrayals.

Senator Vasquez, aware of his fragile position, initiated a series of behind-the-scenes meetings. He sought to build solid alliances but knew that loyalty in politics was as ephemeral as the tide. Meanwhile, the President's daughter, Isabella, silently observed, aware of the power her influence could wield over political destinies.

Amidst this turmoil, a new player entered the stage. The enigmatic political consultant, Alejandro Mendez, whose skills were as obscure as his motives. His presence added an additional layer of complexity to the game, and his silent influence began to spread through the corridors of power.

Alliances formed and dissolved, like waves breaking on the beach. Each character, guided by personal ambitions, navigated this stormy sea of politics, aware that a single wrong move could mean their downfall.

As the curtain rose more, the stage of power transformed into a chessboard where each piece was crucial. Intrigues and alliances intertwined, and characters moved like pawns in a dangerous game, where victory was uncertain, and consequences were unpredictable.

CHAPTER 3
THE GAME OF MANIPULATION

While political backstage boiled, the game of manipulation gained intensity. In the corridors of power, secrets were whispered, and each word had the potential to trigger a chain reaction. Alejandro Mendez, the shadowy political consultant, revealed his expertise in the art of manipulation, weaving intricate webs to achieve his goals.

Senator Vasquez, now involved in an unstable alliance, began to perceive the machinations around him. However, he also learned to play the game, using information strategically to consolidate his power. The political board was in constant flux, and the ability to anticipate moves became a valuable weapon.

Isabella, the President's daughter, found herself in the center of an elaborate plot. Her growing influence made her both a valuable asset and a target for those who coveted her power. Every interaction, every choice, shaped the destinies of the characters, creating a complex web of relationships and rivalries.

While the curtains of power continued to rise, the characters discovered that, in the game of manipulation, the truth was often as malleable as morality. The quest for control led to unexpected twists, and those who underestimated the power of manipulation were caught off guard.

In the next act of this political saga, the stage of power would be the scene of revelations and betrayals, where the true architects of manipulation would emerge from the shadows.

CHAPTER 4
BETWEEN LINES AND ALLIANCES

In the unfolding drama of power, the lines between allies and adversaries blurred. Loyalties were tested, and alliances became increasingly fragile. The President, sensing the shifting dynamics, sought to solidify his position by forming unexpected alliances with influential figures.

Senator Vasquez, torn between conflicting loyalties, faced the dilemma of choosing between personal principles and political survival. The choices made in the shadows had consequences that rippled through the intricate tapestry of the political landscape.

Isabella, burdened by the weight of her influence, grappled with the realization that every alliance came at a cost. The game of power demanded sacrifices, and the currency of influence was paid in the currency of personal relationships.

Amidst the chaos, Alejandro Mendez continued to pull the strings from the shadows. His motivations remained elusive, and his maneuvers added an air of unpredictability to the political chessboard. As alliances shifted, the characters found themselves navigating a maze of deception and intrigue.

Between lines written and alliances forged, the stage of power transformed into a battleground where trust was a rare commodity. The characters, entangled in the complex web of politics, faced the harsh reality that in the pursuit of power, sacrifices were inevitable.

CHAPTER 5
CONSPIRACIES AND TWISTS

As the political drama unfolded, conspiracies and twists emerged like dark shadows in the corridors of power. The alliances forged in the crucible of political necessity now faced the test of hidden agendas and covert schemes.

President Martinez, recognizing the fragility of his alliances, initiated a series of strategic maneuvers. Behind closed doors, he navigated the treacherous waters of political conspiracies, where trust was a luxury and betrayal a constant companion.

Senator Vasquez, caught in the crossfire of conflicting interests, discovered that his attempts to play both sides came with a heavy price. The whispers of conspiracy grew louder, and the lines between friend and foe became increasingly blurred.

Isabella, aware of the looming conspiracies, grappled with the weight of her influence. Her choices held the power to shape the destiny of the nation, but each decision came with the risk of manipulation and betrayal.

Alejandro Mendez, the elusive puppet master, reveled in the chaos he orchestrated. His influence extended like a web, ensnaring the unsuspecting players in a game where the rules were ever-changing.

In this chapter of political intrigue, the characters faced not only external threats but also the internal turmoil of their own ambitions. The stage of power, now a breeding ground for conspiracies, set the scene for a series of twists that would redefine the balance of political forces.

CHAPTER 6
THE STORM APPROACHES

A storm was brewing on the horizon, and the stage of power trembled with anticipation. The intricate dance of politics reached a crescendo as external forces, unseen and unpredictable, threatened to reshape the landscape.

President Martinez, realizing the imminent storm, sought to consolidate his power. The alliances he had forged were now put to the ultimate test as the tempest of political upheaval loomed on the horizon.

Senator Vasquez, caught in the crosscurrents of power, faced the challenge of navigating the storm. The choices made in the calm would determine whether he emerged unscathed or succumbed to the turbulent forces at play.

Isabella, sensing the impending storm, grappled with the responsibility that came with her influence. The decisions she made could either weather the storm or intensify its fury, and the weight of her choices rested heavily on her shoulders.

Alejandro Mendez, the puppet master of political machinations, reveled in the chaos. The storm was his canvas, and the manipulation of its forces his art. As the characters braced for impact, the true extent of his influence would be revealed.

In the eye of the storm, the stage of power transformed into a battleground where survival depended on adaptability and foresight. The characters, entangled in the turbulent currents of politics, faced a challenge that would redefine the course of their destinies.

CHAPTER 7
FRAGILE ALLIANCES

The storm had arrived, and the alliances that once seemed unbreakable now faced the test of survival. In the corridors of power, trust was a scarce commodity, and loyalty hung by a fragile thread.

President Martinez, grappling with the forces of the storm, found himself surrounded by shifting allegiances. The political landscape, once stable, now resembled a battlefield where every move carried the risk of betrayal.

Senator Vasquez, torn between conflicting loyalties, navigated the treacherous waters of political intrigue. The alliances he had forged were now his only lifelines in the storm, and each decision became a calculated gamble.

Isabella, caught in the crossfire of political turmoil, confronted the harsh reality of her influence. The power she held became both a shield and a target, and the choices made in the chaos would determine the fate of the nation.

Alejandro Mendez, the elusive puppet master, continued to pull strings in the shadows. The storm was his playground, and the chaos his ally. As alliances crumbled and new ones formed, the true extent of his influence became increasingly apparent.

In this chapter of fragile alliances, the characters faced the harsh truth that, in the storm of power, survival depended on adaptability and the ability to navigate the shifting currents. The stage of power, once a symbol of authority, now stood as a testament to the impermanence of alliances in the face of political tempests.

CHAPTER 8
PERSONAL CONFLICTS

Amidst the political storm, personal conflicts emerged like cracks in the facade of power. The characters, grappling with their own demons, found themselves entangled in a web of emotions that threatened to unravel the carefully woven tapestry of politics.

President Martinez, burdened by the weight of leadership, confronted the personal conflicts that came with the pursuit of power. The choices made in the crucible of crisis revealed the true character of the man behind the presidential mask.

Senator Vasquez, torn between duty and personal values, faced a moral dilemma that transcended the political storm. The decisions that once seemed black and white now blurred into shades of gray, and the line between right and wrong became increasingly elusive.

Isabella, caught in the crossfire of personal and political conflicts, grappled with the consequences of her choices. The power she wielded came at a cost, and the toll on her personal relationships became evident as the storm raged on.

Alejandro Mendez, the puppet master of manipulation, confronted his own inner conflicts. The motives that drove his actions were shrouded in mystery, and the storm became a mirror reflecting the complexity of his own psyche.

As the characters faced personal conflicts amidst the political turmoil, the stage of power transformed into a battlefield of emotions. The true test of character unfolded in the midst of crisis, where personal convictions clashed with the demands of political survival.

CHAPTER 9
INTERTWINED BETRAYALS

As the protagonists navigated the treacherous waters of politics, betrayals began to intertwine in unpredictable ways. Once-solid alliances trembled in the face of surprising revelations, challenging the loyalty of characters whose motivations remained hidden.

The political scandal unfolding on the stage of power was not merely a battle of ideas and strategies; it was a war of meticulously planned betrayals. Conspirators were revealed, while others remained in the shadows, weaving a complex web of deceit.

Isabella, in her quest for truth, found herself entangled in an intricate plot of lies and betrayals. Each step towards the light revealed a deeper shadow, and the lines between allies and enemies became increasingly blurred.

Vasquez, in turn, discovered that trusting those around him was a risky task. His closest advisors revealed hidden agendas, and he found himself on a chessboard where the pieces were moved by personal interests rather than loyalty to the country.

In the ninth chapter of 'The Curtain Rises,' intertwined betrayals formed a complex web, threatening not only the destinies of the protagonists but also the fragile balance of power that kept society on the brink of chaos.

CHAPTER 10
UNVEILING IN THE SHADOWS

The curtain finally lifted, revealing the dark contours of the true power game. At the height of betrayals and revelations, the fates of the protagonists became inextricably intertwined with the fate of the nation.

Isabella, now aware of the betrayals surrounding her journey, confronted the architects of the shadows. The past collided with the present, revealing a network of conspiracies that spanned decades. In her quest for justice, Isabella faced impossible choices, where the price of truth was too high.

Vasquez, on the other hand, confronted his own demons. The leadership he had sought so fervently proved to be a heavy burden, laden with the consequences of choices made behind the scenes of power. Amidst the political chaos, he had to decide whether truth should be sacrificed for the sake of stability.

In the unveiling in the shadows, the lines between right and wrong, truth and falsehood, became blurred. The protagonists, marked by betrayals and difficult choices, found themselves facing a new dawn, where the stage of power would continue to be fertile ground for political dramas, intrigues, and above all, the eternal dance between light and shadows.